HAL LEONARD KEYBOARD STYLE SERIES

STRIDE & SWING
PIANO

THE COMPLETE GUIDE WITH CD!

BY JOHN VALERIO

ISBN 978-0-634-04663-6

HAL•LEONARD®
CORPORATION

7777 W. BLUEMOUND RD. P.O. BOX 13819 MILWAUKEE, WI 53213

In Australia Contact:
Hal Leonard Australia Pty. Ltd.
22 Taunton Drive P.O. Box 5130
Cheltenham East, 3192 Victoria, Australia
Email: ausadmin@halleonard.com

Visit Hal Leonard Online at www.halleonard.com

INTRODUCTION

Welcome to *Stride and Swing Piano*! This book is an in-depth look at early solo jazz piano styles from the 1900s to the 1940s. Many pianists know the term *stride* as an accompaniment technique in which the left hand alternates between a bass note and a chord in an "oom-pah, oom-pah" manner. But stride was also the label given to a style of piano music that emerged in the 1920s. This was an early form of jazz that evolved from predecessors like ragtime, blues, and New Orleans style, and culminated in the *swing* style of the 1930s and '40s. Most of the early jazz piano styles up to and including swing piano feature this striding left-hand motion.

This book traces the evolution of stride and swing piano styles—from their predecessors to their fullest development; each chapter focuses on a particular style and player:

Classic Ragtime: Though not jazz per se, ragtime was an important forerunner, serving as a model for styles like New Orleans and stride. Invented by Black Americans, ragtime emerged during the 1890s and was a strictly written music with formal and rhythmic constraints. Scott Joplin was its most famous composer.

Blues & Boogie Woogie: Also invented by Black Americans (in the 1800s), blues was another important forerunner of stride and swing jazz styles. A looser music, blues had its own melodic material, accompaniment style, and rhythmic feel. Jimmy Yancey was a premiere blues pianist; Pete Johnson was a well-known player in the faster, boogie woogie style.

New Orleans Jazz: In the early 1900s, New Orleans pianists developed jazz, a style that merged ragtime with blues, and added improvisation. Jelly Roll Morton was the most important early jazz pianist. He loosened the "even subdivisions" of ragtime and made jazz swing.

Stride: Stride was a fast, virtuosic piano music born in Harlem during the 1920s and '30s. Early stride, à la James P. Johnson, was more appropriately called "Eastern ragtime" than later stride, which evolved into a lighter, smoother music, as played by Fats Waller.

Swing: Swing emerged during the mid '30s with jazz big bands. The driving accents of stride were ironed out, and an even 4/4 pulse became the norm. Teddy Wilson best represented the swing style; Art Tatum took it to its highest point.

The one element that all of these styles have in common is the almost continuous playing of the pulse (on every beat) by the left hand. This was accomplished by: 1) bass note vs. chord alternation, 2) the playing of bass lines, or 3) the continuous playing of chords.

Modern jazz piano styles have done away with the left hand's time keeping role for the most part, and contemporary players are often at a loss when called upon to play the left hand in an older solo style. *Stride and Swing Piano* offers an introduction to the usage of traditional left-hand devices—including characteristic chord voicings and bass note intervals, such as octaves and tenths—as well as right-hand techniques such as single-note lines, chord voicings, intervals, runs, and improvisation. Each chapter culminates in one or more original tunes demonstrating the style and its techniques. Practice suggestions are also included. The reader is encouraged to learn and study these tunes, and to apply all of the techniques in the book to standard jazz and pop songs of the era.

About the CD

The accompanying CD features many of the examples in the book—including 14 original tunes—performed on solo piano. Listen to the CD to better understand each style and to practice your own solo playing.

CONTENTS

Chapter One

CLASSIC RAGTIME
SCOTT JOPLIN

Ragtime was created by Black Americans in the 1890s and gained widespread popularity by 1900. Though not jazz per se, ragtime was an important forerunner of jazz. Practically all jazz piano styles until the 1940s were based on the ragtime model. In fact, several early jazz piano styles were still referred to as ragtime, and because of this the term "classic ragtime" is used to distinguish the original version from later versions such as "Eastern ragtime."

Scott Joplin (1868-1917) is the most famous and most popular classic ragtime composer. The succeeding description is based largely on his work. Others include James Scott and Joseph Lamb. Unlike later jazz styles, the classic ragtime composers thought of their music as formal compositions in the European tradition and did not improvise or alter them very much during performance.

History & Evolution

Ragtime is unique in that it represents the first formal blending of European and West African musical elements. The form and harmony came from Europe; the rhythmic concept came from West Africa.

The Cakewalk and The March

Ragtime evolved primarily from two musical styles: the cakewalk and the march. The *cakewalk* was a dance originally performed by slaves on plantations in the South. It featured high, strutting movements that mocked the slave owner's pompous walk and attitude, and was usually accompanied by a kind of syncopated music on a banjo. A characteristic melodic rhythm, syncopated and repetitive, developed. (Syncopations are marked with asterisks.)

By the late 1800s, published cakewalks appeared in the form of piano music. The right-hand part featured the rhythm shown above; the left hand featured a steady bass-note/chord alternation, derived from the *march*. This fairly constant "oom-pah, oom-pah" motion became characteristic of published cakewalks. A typical left-hand part is shown below.

Thus the seeds of ragtime were sowed: a syncopated-like right hand played against a steady left-hand pulse. Ragtime, however, was more complex than the cakewalk. Its rhythmic complexity is not easily explained by European concepts like syncopation.

The West African Influence

Ragtime is actually a simplification of traditional West African rhythmic practice, based on the concept of *layering*. West African drum music usually features several meters going on at the same time. This polymetic music is quite complex compared to European metric practice. Whereas typical European music follows a single meter usually limited to groupings in twos, threes, and fours (e.g., 2/4, 3/4, 4/4, etc.), it is not uncommon for West African music to proceed with several different meters played by different musicians at the same time. Thus, in European terms, there might be 3/4, 4/4, 5/4, 7/4, and 9/4 going on simultaneously.

TRACK 1

Ragtime was conceived on two simultaneous layers of rhythmic activity. The left hand kept a steady four beats per measure by alternating a bass note and chord. The right hand played melodies based on a pulse of eight beats per measure—twice the speed of the left. The right-hand melodies were grouped into patterns based on the African concept of *additive rhythms*. Rhythmic groupings and accent patterns such as 3+3+2 or 3+3+3 were played by the right hand while the steady four beats per measure were played by the left hand at half the speed. This led to many accented notes played by the right hand that did not coincide with the beats played by the left. The effect to Western ears was one of syncopation, but the real rhythmic concept should be understood as separate simultaneous layers. An example of a typical ragtime segment (3+3+2 pattern) follows.

This had important ramifications for jazz, which evolved into a rhythmically multi-layered music. The key elementsof ragtime that carried over into early jazz piano was this rhythmic conception, as well as the basic left-hand technique that went with it.

Left Hand Techniques

In classic ragtime, the left hand keeps the pulse by playing a steady beat consisting of four equal subdivisions of the 2/4 meter. Continuous steady eighth notes are the norm. The normal left-hand material consists primarily of bass notes and chords, which usually, although not always, alternate in a bass note/chord pattern, commonly referred to as "oom-pah." Thus, the left hand typically plays "oom-pah, oom-pah," etc.

This oom-pah motion was later referred to as "stride" because of the striding back-and-forth motion of the left hand. (The term "stride piano" was later used to describe one of the jazz outgrowths of classic ragtime.) The striding left hand performs three different functions; it supplies the pulse, the bass, and the harmony. It is important that the player of ragtime is aware of these separate functions as he or she performs in this style.

Pulse, Meter, and Tempo

Traditional ragtime was written in 2/4 time and conceived in "2," with two beats per measure. Thus, although the left hand in ragtime plays four steady eighth notes per measure, they are not all equal in stress. The notes occurring on the beats receive more stress that the notes in between the beats, the offbeats. This distinction is important when replicating true ragtime as opposed to jazz (which is conceived in 4/4, with four beats per measure).

True ragtime tempos are never fast and are usually played at moderate march-like speeds. Scott Joplin used tempos marks such as: *Tempo di marcia* and *Not fast.* Most rags should be played between ♩ = 92-108

Chords

The chords used in classic ragtime are relatively simple. For the most part, they're confined to major and minor triads, and dominant and diminished seventh chords. The chords are usually played on the offbeats—called "after-chords"—and consist of three notes. Any inversion is possible; however, some positions are more likely for certain chords due to range limitations. The chord tones usually go no lower than D below middle C and no higher than A above middle C.

The following example shows the most commonly used three-note major triad voicings. The same positions apply to the minor triads built from the same roots.

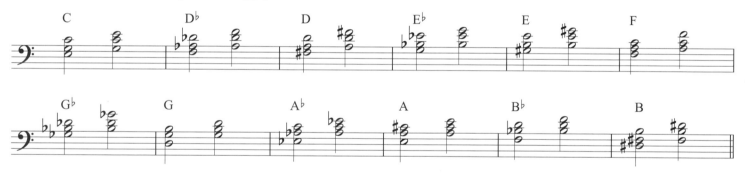

Although dominant seventh chords are four-note chords, one note (usually the fifth) is often eliminated from the chord to form a three-note voicing. The common three-note seventh chord voicings for all dominant seventh chords are given below.

Voice Leading

Though alternated with bass notes, chords typically connect to each other with the smoothest voice leading possible, i.e. with the least movement from chord to chord. Smooth chord connection is demonstrated in the next example by separating each chord from its bass note.

Bass Notes

Bass notes are chosen to best establish the tonality and harmonic movement of the music and to give the bass line a sense of direction. The most common bass note is the root of the chord. When a chord's duration is longer than one beat (which it usually is), the next bass note is usually the fifth or less commonly the third.

- The third is most often used to provide a stepwise bass line to connect chords.
- When the root of one chord would cause a repetition of the previously used bass note, the fifth is usually played first, then the root.

The following example demonstrates these principles.

Sometimes, the after-chord contains only two notes of a triad. This can be for textural variety or practical considerations of voice leading and register. In most cases, the missing note is supplied by the bass. In the following example, the basic chords are shown in the upper stave.

Bass notes are often reinforced with octaves. Density and balance of sound are determining factors in choosing octaves or single notes for the bass part.

Diminished Chords

Diminished chords are used in classic ragtime. Most often, the root is played as a bass note and the remaining three notes are played in the after-chord. Diminished seventh chords are most commonly found in cadential progressions that end a section of music.

"Oom-Pah" Variations

Variety is added to the left-hand part through the following ways:

1. Reverse the bass-note/chord pattern to chord/bass-note (oom-pah, pah-oom).

2. Play two or more bass notes in a row (passing notes or otherwise).

3. Play several chords in a row without bass notes (often these are four-note voicings of triads or seventh chords).

4. Play quasi-melodic material along with or independent from the right hand.

5. Play rhythms that depart from the eighth-note pulse.

The previous left-hand techniques represent the most common procedures. There are other possibilities, and almost anything can occur in the left-hand part.

Right-Hand Techniques

Rhythmic Layering

As discussed previously, the true essence of ragtime lies in the layering concept of rhythm. The right hand functions on a layer or stratum independent from the left. Metrically, the left hand operates on a layer of four pulses per measure, while the right hand operates on a layer of eight pulses per measure. This concept of multi-meters operating at the same time, when properly understood, can clarify the way ragtime works.

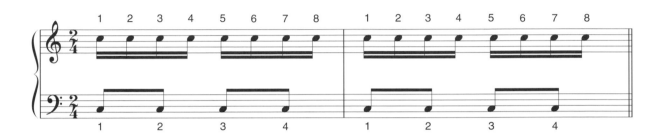

Whereas the left hand almost always states its pulse directly by playing continuous eighth notes, the right hand plays melodies based on its sixteenth-note pulse, employing a variety of rhythms. The rhythms of these melodies sound very syncopated in relation to the left-hand pulse since many of the stressed or accented notes fall in between. Below is an example of a typical ragtime right-hand melodic rhythm in relation to the steady left-hand pulse. The RH accents and dotted lines show the syncopation effect.

The next example shows the left-hand/right-hand relationship taken from the first strain of Scott Joplin's "The Entertainer." Notice that right-hand stresses occur both on and in between the left-hand pulses.

Although by traditional Western music standards this seems like syncopation, what's really going on is the West African concept of additive rhythms. The right hand stresses are based on accent patterns of groupings of the sixteenth-note pulse. Typical groupings are 3+3+2 or 3+3+3 patterns. The next example shows both of these patterns as sixteenth note groupings in the upper staff, with the full value of each grouping indicated in the middle staff. The left-hand pulse is indicated on the lower staff.

One can hear the effect of this rhythmic layering by tapping or clapping the left-hand pulse against the right-hand patterns, either as sixteenth notes with accents, or the full durational value of each grouping.

The next example shows the rhythmic breakdown of a section of Scott Joplin's "Maple Leaf Rag." There are two 3+3+3+3 groupings separated by a group of 4. The essence of ragtime rhythmic layering can be heard by tapping, clapping, or singing the layers against each other.

Ragtime's rhythms can also be related to its predecessor, the cakewalk. By adding notes to a basic cakewalk rhythm, and tying some of them, a cross-rhythmic layering effect is created.

Melody & Texture

Ragtime melodies are based on simple diatonic scales and generally are more interesting for their rhythmic quality than their pure melodic motions. Ragtime compositions are usually in major keys. These keys are generally limited to C, G, F, B♭, E♭, A♭, and D♭. The textures used in the right hand include single notes, octaves, filled-in octaves, two-note intervals, and chords. The arrangement of these various textures is often but not always determined by the rhythmic structure of the melody. In the following excerpt, adding notes to the single-note melody emphasizes the right-hand syncopations.

The choice among the various textural possibilities is often just a matter of density or variety. In the excerpt below, the thick texture of the first two measures is in sharp contrast with the following two measures.

Harmony and Form

Most rags are written in sectional forms derived from march forms. Rags generally contain three or four sixteen-measure strains. Each strain is self-contained, and rarely do their melodies relate to each other. Typical forms break down as follows: AABBCC, AABBCCDD, AABBACCDD. The C section is called the "trio," a term borrowed from traditional marches and dance forms. It has nothing to do with the instrumentation but refers to a contrasting section usually in a contrasting key, most often the subdominant. Some rags stay in the new key for the succeeding section, and some rags even change keys in each new section.

The harmonic progressions are relatively simple with I, IV, and V7 chords predominating. Chromaticism is supplied mostly through diminished seventh and secondary dominant chords. Scott Joplin also used chromatically altered chords, most commonly a minor triad built on IV, and chords built on ♭VI either as triads or augmented sixth chords (essentially dominant seventh chords built on the ♭VI degree of the major scale).

The harmonic rhythm is generally slow with each chord usually lasting for one or two measures. Harmonic change often comes quicker toward cadences. Inversions are used for variety and to smooth out bass lines. Typically, each sixteen-measure strain contains four phrases. The second phrase usually ends on a half cadence on V. Below is the chord progression of the second strain of Scott Joplin's "The Entertainer."

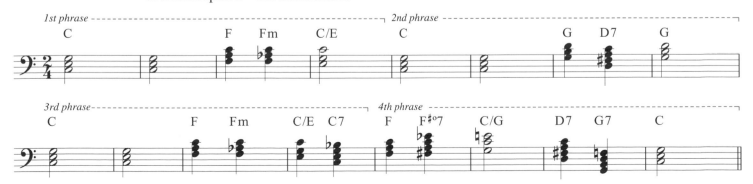

"Any Old Rag"

"Any Old Rag" represents the classic ragtime tradition. The form is AABBCCDD. It is in the key of C major. The C section, the trio, is in the subdominant key of F major. The right hand plays various additive rhythm groupings that often do not coincide with the steady pulse of the left hand. Notice the use of chromatic chords toward the final cadence of each strain. Be careful to play this and all classic rags in a moderate tempo and with evenness in both hands. Classic ragtime should not swing in the modern sense of the word.

TRACK 4

John Valerio

PRACTICE SUGGESTIONS

As with most piano styles, "separate hands" practice is recommended for ragtime. The left hand in particular needs to keep a steady pulse while providing a fairly constant oom-pah motion. Practice simple stride patterns first before attempting those that are more complex—the simplest patterns involve the least hand movement. All of the patterns that follow should be practiced in strict tempo, ranging from the slowest comfortable tempo to ♩ = 100.

Left Hand (Simple)

The simplest pattern for a major triad is shown here for a I chord in the key of C, followed by one for the V7 chord (G7) and one for the IV chord (F). Practice these patterns individually at first.

Once the patterns are somewhat comfortable, try to connect them.

Invent other chord progressions using I, IV, and V7 chords, and practice them repeatedly. Practice the patterns in other keys, too—especially G, F, B♭, E♭, A♭, and D♭ major.

Left Hand (Complex)

Once simple stride patterns have been mastered, try more difficult ones with larger leaps. Separate patterns for I, IV, and V7 in C major follow.

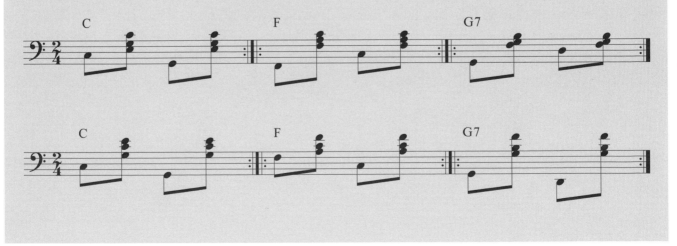

These patterns can be combined in various ways. Notice the smooth chord connections.

Be sure to practice patterns using the thirds of chords as bass notes.

Once you feel comfortable with the previous patterns, try using octaves for bass notes.

Both Hands

Since classic ragtime relies on two separate rhythmic layers, coordinating the two hands can be difficult. The following exercises address this problem.

Sixteenth notes played by the right hand should be evenly played as equal subdivisions of the eighth notes played by the left hand. Practice the following exercises, at first with no accents, then with the 3+3+2 and 3+3+3 accent patterns shown. Strive for precision.

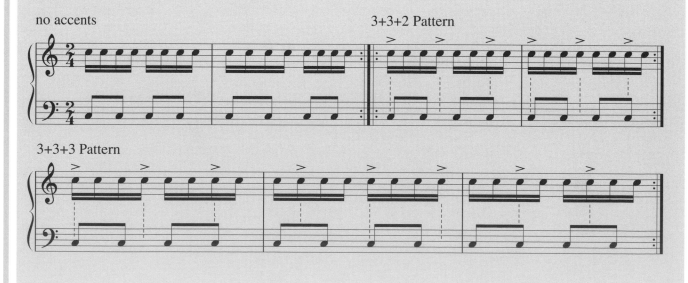

The previous accent patterns can also be reduced to their full value and played as follows.

3+3+2 Pattern   3+3+3 Pattern

Abstract the right-hand and left-hand rhythms of written rags and practice them as above, as in this example from Scott Joplin.

Then try adding chords and octaves.

The 3+3+2 and the 3+3+3, or any other patterns, can be practiced with a striding left hand.

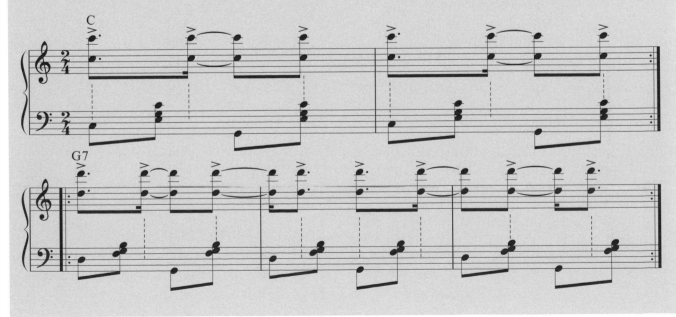

Chapter Two
BLUES & BOOGIE WOOGIE
JIMMY YANCEY & PETE JOHNSON

Another immediate forerunner of jazz was *blues*. Like ragtime, blues was invented by Black Americans—originating on Southern plantations during the mid-nineteenth century—and represented a fusion of Western and African musical elements. Originally a vocal music, blues was characterized by an expressive inflection of pitch that made use of bending, sliding, and "singing in the cracks," i.e., singing pitches in between the tempered notes of the scale. Rhythmically, blues melodies were also very supple and flexible; the note values did not easily break down into units like quarter notes, eighth notes, etc. The accompaniment, on the other hand, always had a strong sense of beat and supplied the pulse. This, as in ragtime, gave a layering effect—but the melodic layer was more independent from the pulse layer since it was not restricted to even subdivision of the basic pulse.

Blues piano developed in the early 1900s. Pianists, of course, could not bend notes or play in the cracks, but they developed ways simulating these effects. A characteristic scale known as the blues scale became common for melodies, while traditional Western harmonic practice prevailed for the accompaniment. Thus, we see another example of layering, this time involving two separate tonal planes. In the 1920s, faster versions of piano blues emerged know as *boogie woogie*.

Blues Piano

The Blues Scale

Traditional blues melodies are based on the so-called *blues* scale—a five-note, "pentatonic," scale superimposed on a major tonality. In many traditional blues performances, the five-note blues scale provides all of the melodic material. In others, it's mixed in with the major scale. More modern practice adds a sixth note, the flat fifth (G♭), to the traditional pentatonic.

Traditional Blues Scale

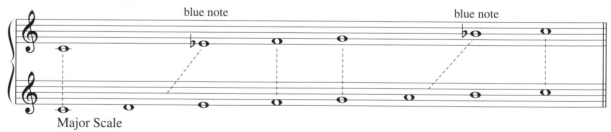

Major Scale

Modern Blues Scale

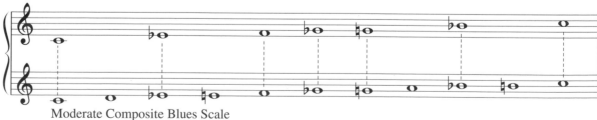

Moderate Composite Blues Scale

The flat third and flat seventh (e.g., E♭ and B♭) are known as *blue notes*. It should be noted that these blue notes were actually somewhere between the natural and flatted pitches (E and E♭, for instance) and can never be replicated exactly on a piano.

Crushed and Grace Notes

Most early blues pianists made use of a composite blues scale. Blue notes were used as inflected flatted notes, and often the major and minor third were crushed together for a characteristic blues effect. Often, the minor third was used as a grace note to inflect the major third. Grace note ornaments and crush minor seconds were common on other scale degrees, as well. The following examples show some of these characteristic right-hand blues devices.

TRACK 5

Thirds, Sixths, and Tremolos

TRACK 6

The early blues pianists often played parallel 6ths and 3rds in their right hand. Tremolos—rapid alternation between two or more notes wider than a 2nd—were also popular.

Repeated Notes and Patterns

TRACK 7

Often several, or long strings, of repeated notes, intervals, or chords were played.

Swing/Shuffle Rhythm

Whereas classic ragtime was conceived in 2/4 time, blues was conveived in 4/4—that is, four beats per measure. However, many early blues performances featured triplets in the melody and accompaniment, and these performances are often notated in 12/8 time, sometimes referred to as "shuffle." There is a certain influence from the field holler, work song, spiritual, and black gospel music traditions. The feeling of the triplet led to what we now call *swing eighth notes*. What is written as ♫ is played as ♪³♪. The use of swing eighths became standard in jazz during the 1920s.

12-Bar Blues Form

Early blues pianists made much use of the traditional *12-bar blues form*. Several variations on the basic chord progression were used, but the basic form remained intact. To this day, it serves as a remarkably flexible and versatile form. The chords were quite simple: triads and dominant seventh chords. Three typical early blues chord progressions follow below, in the key of C.

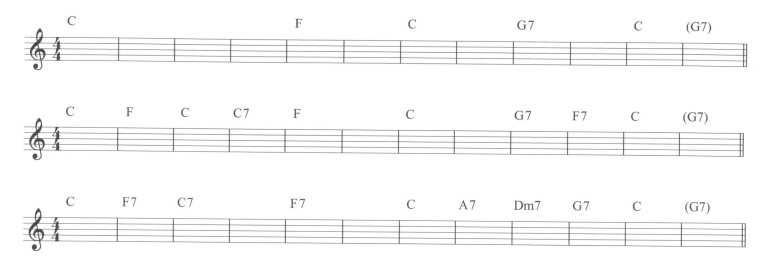

The unique tonal quality present in traditional blues comes from the clash between the melody and accompaniment. The harmonic accompaniment is based solely on the major scale, while the melodies are based on blues scales. The blue notes clash with their counterparts in the major scale. In C, for instance, the E♭/E♮ and B♭/B♮ clash. These clashes create a certain tension that is associated with "the blues."

Traditional blues vocal melodies and lyrics followed the form of AAB. In this form, there are three four-measure phrases. The first phrase is repeated more or less exactly (words and melody) even though the harmony is different the second time. The third phrase is usually different from the first two and acts as a kind of punch line. The repeated melody and words add a certain amount of tension to the performances, and the third, "punch line" phrase relieves that tension. Early instrumental blues tunes did not necessarily adhere to that melodic form, in large part because of the lack of words.

Left-Hand Patterns

TRACK 8

Early blues piano playing featured simple repetitive single-note accompaniments in the left hand. A few samples follow.

Early blues piano playing was a bit more formal than its vocal counterpart, but much less formal than classic ragtime. (Blues tunes were rarely written down until after 1910, and unlike classic rag, improvisation was and is a key factor in blues performances.) As for most jazz performances, notation does not capture every nuance of rhythm and feeling. The reader should notice the simpler more "laid back" character that early blues has compared to classic ragtime.

"Nothin' Fancy"

Jimmy Yancey (1894-1951) was an early blues pianist whose early style remained pure and simple. His approach represents a blues style unaffected by the influence of ragtime. He also became influential in the boogie woogie style of the 1920s. The following tune is written in his pure blues style. Other blues pianists include Clarence "Pinetop" Smith and Roosevelt Sykes.

TRACK 9

John Valerio

PRACTICE SUGGESTIONS

Blues left-hand patterns should be practiced alone before playing them with the right hand.

- Take any or all of the left-hand patterns shown and play them slowly at first; then gradually increase the speed.
- Next, play simple improvisations based on the blues scale with the right hand along with the left-hand patterns.
- Next, improvise using the blues scale and major scale while playing characteristic blues devices—like crushed and grace notes, thirds, sixths, and tremolos, and repeated notes and patterns.

Follow a similar procedure when practicing boogie-woogie-style blues piano.

Boogie Woogie

Boogie woogie is a subcategory of blues piano, characterized by fast tempos and virtuosic displays. This style flourished and became very popular during the 1920s. Although originally a medium for solo piano, swing bands began to incorporate boogie woogie into many of their arrangements during the 1930s and '40s. In the '50s, boogie woogie became a major influence on rock 'n' roll, especially rock 'n' roll pianists.

Left-Hand Patterns

TRACK 10

A crucial rhythmic element of boogie woogie is the feeling of eight beats per measure—the saying, "Beat me, daddy, eight to the bar," was a familiar call in boogie woogie's heyday. An eighth-note pulse superimposed on 4/4 time creates another layer of rhythmic activity, crucial for defining boogie woogie. These patterns should be played crisply with a heavy swing feeling.

Right-Hand Techniques

Boogie woogie melodies typically consist of short, repetitive, catchy phrases. Much of the right-hand material is similar to that of blues piano: blues scale, grace notes, crushed seconds, thirds, sixths, and tremolos. Boogie pianists also emphasized fourths.

TRACK 11

Repeated notes and repeated short patterns of notes were typically employed.

Polyrhythms were often used, creating cross-rhythmic effects.

TRACK 12

TRACK 13

Boogie woogie melodies featured short repetitive riff-like patterns. Two examples follow.

"Boogie Man's Blues"

Pete Johnson (1904-1967) was one of the premiere boogie woogie pianists of the 1920s and '30s. A virtuoso who anticipated many of the rock 'n' roll piano styles of the '50s, Johnson teamed up with vocalist Joe Turner in the '30s and produced prototypical rhythm 'n' blues/rock 'n' roll recordings. Other prominent boogie woogie pianists were Meade "Lux" Lewis and Albert Ammons.

"Boogie Man's Blues" is written in Pete Johnson's style. It consists of three blues choruses. The beginning of the first chorus acts as an introduction—one that was imitated by many '50s rock 'n' roll pianists. The first two choruses use the same left-hand boogie pattern; the third chorus uses a different pattern. Notice the repetitive riff-like figures and the use of thirds and fourths in the right hand. Also, notice the repeated notes and repetitive chromatic figures. The tempo is fairly fast, so one should gradually build up speed, and practice each hand separately before attempting them together.

TRACK 14

John Valerio

Chapter Three
NEW ORLEANS JAZZ
JELLY ROLL MORTON

Around the year 1900, a new kind of "syncopated" music was born in New Orleans. It was called *jazz*. Elements of blues and other traditional African American music—such as spirituals, field hollers, and work songs—merged with elements of classic ragtime and march music to create a different and unique musical genre. In many ways, jazz resembled classic ragtime, but its feel, sound, and methods were very different. Whereas ragtime was strict, jazz was loose; whereas ragtime was written down, jazz was improvised.

Jelly Roll Morton (1885-1941) was one of the first and most prominent pianists to play in what can truly be called a jazz style, and was the first great arranger/composer in the genre. Other than playing solo, Morton led one of the top New Orleans style (Dixieland) bands, the Red Hot Peppers. One immediately noticeable difference between his music and classic ragtime is that Morton's music *swings*. He loosened the "even subdivisions" effect of ragtime—turning "straight" eighth notes into "swing" eighth notes by playing them unevenly in a long-short manner (♪♪ = ♪♪)—and this more relaxed attitude has stayed with jazz ever since.

Swing relies on more than just the underlying rhythmic feel, however. It's difficult to describe, yet most listeners know it when they hear it. Swing relates to subtle shadings of dynamics and accents, as well as rhythmic placement. It relates to a "going against the grain" quality that applies not only to rhythm, but also to harmony and melody as they relate to pulse, meter, cadence, form, and each other. Whereas classic ragtime was in 2/4 time, jazz is in 4/4. This is an important difference. Ragtime adheres to a system of strong beats and weak beats—the bass notes (1 and 2) are emphasized, while the after-chords (the "and"s) are significantly weaker. In jazz, the bass notes are played on beats 1 and 3, and after-chords on beats 2 and 4; thus, the after-chords occur on the beat level, not as after-beats. Essentially, there are no weak beats in jazz. Jazz makes all the beats equal on the melodic and pulse levels, and any beat can be stressed. Often beats 2 and 4, or even the "and"s in between the beats, are stressed. This equalization of all beats gives jazz its basic underpinning for swinging. The harmonic structure generally adheres to the traditional procedure of changing on the "strong" beats, 1 and 3, but rhythmically, jazz goes against this grain.

The following example shows the difference between classic ragtime and jazz regarding the pulse.

TRACK 15

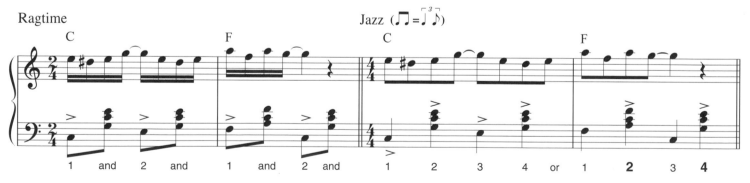

Left-Hand Techniques

Jelly Roll Morton extended the left-hand techniques of classic ragtime, utilizing all the basic devices—the left hand kept the pulse as before, and the basic "oom-pah" bass-note/chord alternation was the norm—while adding new twists all his own. He advanced the art of ragtime in one sense, while creating a newer style, jazz.

Chords

Morton's harmonic vocabulary was similar to that of classic ragtime—essentially triads, dominant seventh chords, and diminished sevenths. However, his seventh chord voicings tended to be fuller, using all four notes instead of just three. These can be added to the triad voicings of classic ragtime (see Chapter 1) to create a basic Morton chord vocabulary.

Bass Notes

As in classic ragtime, Morton most often used single notes and octaves as bass notes—with octaves predominating, in Morton's case. However, he also incorporated other intervals—like fifths, sixths, sevenths, and tenths—and even three-note groupings, including all inversions of close-position triads as well as "filled-in" intervals like root-fifth-octave, or root-fifth-tenth.

Keep in mind that the term "bass notes" in this context refers to the "oom" part of the "oom-pah" stride pattern. The following examples show how these are used in Morton's playing.

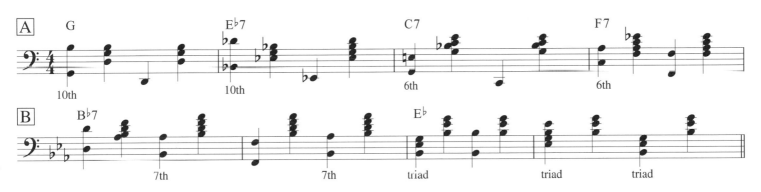

Morton used root-fifth or root-fifth-octave bass groupings in some unorthodox ways. The role of the fifth in these situations is simply to reinforce the overtones of the bass note and otherwise bears no direct relationship to the harmony at that moment. Examples of these unusual fifths are marked by asterisks in the excerpt below.

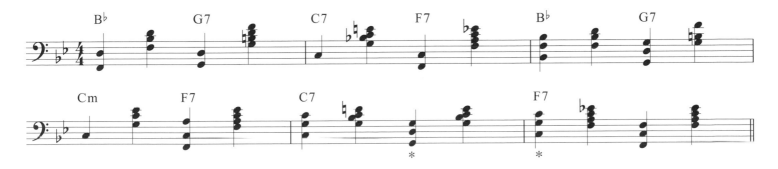

As in classic ragtime, the early jazz piano players connected the after-chords with smooth voice leading. Notice the minimal movement among the after-chords in the previous example.

Walking Bass

Basic striding motion was often broken up with walking bass lines, usually played in single notes or octaves—but tenths and sixths were used as well. These passages could last for one measure or longer. Notice the unusual use of fifths in the second example.

Sometimes, the basic quarter-note rhythm of the left hand was altered by displacing bass notes off the beat and/or running several eighth notes in a row.

Melodic Bass Parts and Breaks

Occasionally, the left hand played lines that were "trombone-like" and/or acted as counter-melodies.

Spanish Rhythms

Jelly Roll claimed that part of the essence of jazz was the "Spanish tinge." Basically this refers to Latin American rhythms, particularly the *habanera* rhythm (♩. ♩. ♩), which is also referred to as the "Charleston rhythm." He sometimes played this rhythm in the left hand as follows.

Half Notes, Whole Notes, Etc.

Sometime the rhythmic activity of the left hand was broken up with sustained chords or intervals. These can be independent from the right hand, or they can be coordinated with it.

Right-Hand Techniques

As mentioned, Jelly Roll Morton swings. He does this by freeing his right hand from his left; the left hand keeps the pulse, and the right hand "floats" freely on top of it. Accents can come anywhere, and often the right hand is in a rhythmic/metric plane different from the left, playing melodic rhythms that cannot be broken down into even subdivisions of the pulse. The subtlety of this rhythmic/metric layering is a hallmark of many great jazz players, including Morton's contemporary, Louis Armstrong. Music notation can only approximate it.

Textures

As in classic ragtime, Morton's right-hand textures included single notes, octaves, filled-in octaves, two-note intervals, and chords. However, Morton used more octaves than ragtime and carefully chose when to add harmony to a melody, sometimes adding the extra notes for textural and harmonic considerations—but more significantly, for rhythmic emphasis. This is similar to the ragtime practice of adding octaves to otherwise single-note melodies, but the effect is slightly different and more subtle. Another technique Morton employed was the tying of one note of a chord into the succeeding chord. This gives a real sense of slurring one melody note into another. The following examples show how these techniques add emphasis to certain notes of the melodic line.

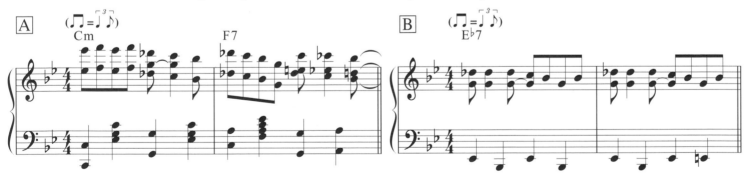

Blues Effects

Morton used various right-hand blues devices, including the blues scale.

Characteristic Melodic Rhythms

Morton used a variety of rhythms in his written and improvised melodies, many derived from classic ragtime. The following example shows rhythm patterns used by both Scott Joplin and Jelly Roll Morton. The only differences are that Joplin's are in 2/4 while Morton's are in 4/4, and Morton's rhythms are swung.

Improvisation

Early New Orleans jazz improvisation was largely based on variation. The given material was altered and embellished in ways that preserved the integrity of the tune by not departing too much from it. Morton adhered to this concept even after Louis Armstrong and others began improvising on chord progressions rather than melodic material. The second chorus of "Jelly Jam Blues" demonstrates a typical improvisational variation on a theme (in this case, the melody of the first chorus).

"Jelly Jam Blues"

For the most part, Morton wrote two types of compositions: blues tunes and longer sectional forms modeled after classic ragtime. "Jelly Jam Blues" is a blues tune in Morton's style. It contains six 12-bar blues choruses. The blues progression used is one of countless variations employed by jazz pianists. The arrangement here is typical of a Morton blues performance, containing elements of both classic ragtime and blues piano.

- The last four measures of each chorus are virtually identical.
- The second chorus is a variation on the first.
- The fifth and sixth choruses are also similar, and function as *shout* choruses. Shout choruses became a standard feature of much early jazz piano; they usually contain *riffs*—short melodic-rhythmic figures that are repeated intact or slightly varied several times throughout a section of the music. The use of riffs became a standard feature of big band music during the Swing era. This produces a driving momentum toward the ending.

Notice the octaves and chords in the right hand serving as accents, the tied notes in the right-hand chords that inflect the melody, the multiple bass notes, the acoustic use of fifths for some bass notes, and the trombone-like counter-melodies in the left hand.

TRACK 16   **Moderately fast Blues**   John Valerio

PRACTICE SUGGESTIONS

New Orleans/Jelly Roll Morton style piano can be practiced in a similar way to classic ragtime. A main difference is that New Orleans style is real jazz and is in 4/4 time, not 2/4.

Left Hand

The left-hand patterns of classic ragtime can be adapted to accommodate Morton's style:

1) Practice basic progressions with fuller dominant seventh chords.

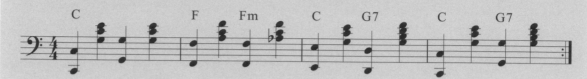

2) Next, add some intervals (or three-note patterns) to the bass notes.

3) Practice common I-IV-V progressions using walking bass lines between chords.

Use any or all of the classic ragtime practice patterns from Ch. 1 and apply similar additions.

Right Hand

Practice typical Morton right-hand textures by creating your own "Jelly Jam Blues" arrangement. First, isolate a particular texture—octaves, for example. Then try mixing textures in a similar way to the given arrangement. Employ fuller sonorities for accents, etc. Also, practice improvising by playing off the blues scale and chords while making variations on the basic melodies of the tune.

Chapter Four

STRIDE PIANO I
JAMES P. JOHNSON

A new style of jazz piano grew out of classic ragtime in the 1920s and early '30s in the Northeast, centered in the Harlem section of New York City. This style is referred to as *Eastern ragtime, Harlem piano school,* or most commonly, *stride piano.* Stride piano evolved in Harlem in the early '20s at "rent parties." These were parties that charged admission to raise rent money. The parties featured cutting contests, where pianists would show off and try to outplay each other for a prize; thus, the music became faster and more complex. A nineteenth-century Black American circle dance called a "ring shout," that featured frenetic dancing, inspired much of this music. (The term *shout piano* comes from this.) Tempos could be extremely fast, and the great stride pianists had amazing left hands that were able to play the steady quarter notes at great speeds. The chords and harmonic progressions were more complex, richer, and fuller than those from classic ragtime, and improvisation was a standard feature of the style. Most important, stride piano *swung.* Like New Orleans jazz, it was conceived in 4/4 rather than 2/4 time.

James P. Johnson (1894-1955) is considered to be the father of stride piano. Like Jelly Roll Morton, he fused elements of classic ragtime and blues to create a pure jazz style that had elements of swing and improvisation. He was classically trained and possessed a virtuoso technique. His playing conveys a sense of forward motion that is associated with jazz rather than classic ragtime. (The term *Eastern ragtime* was used to differentiate this style from the more reserved and staid classic ragtime.) Johnson wrote classical music as well as pop songs such as "Charleston." He earned his main living by making piano rolls for player pianos.

Left-Hand Techniques

Basic Stride

The left-hand techniques used in early stride piano were similar to those used in classic ragtime. However, the chords themselves and the progressions were more complex and more sophisticated in early stride. There was more use of seventh chords, and harmonic rhythms were generally quicker; the duration for each chord was often a half note rather than a whole. Due somewhat to this quicker harmonic rhythm, the bass lines were often stepwise. Below is an example of a typical left-hand segment for an up-tempo shout.

As in classic ragtime, the early stride players usually connected the after-chords with smooth voice leading. Notice the minimal movement among the after-chords above.

Walking Bass

As in New Orleans jazz, the early stride players often broke up the basic stride pattern with walking bass lines. This could last for two or more measures.

Stride players also often displaced the rhythm of a bass line to place the notes off the beats.

Cross-Rhythms

James P. Johnson often attained an interesting cross-rhythmic effect in the left hand by displacing bass notes and after-chords into irregular patterns. The standard "oom-pah" might be tuned into "oom-pah-pah," or "oom-oom-pah," etc. The repetitive use of one of these patterns creates a feeling of 3/4 time superimposed on the basic 4/4 time, thus creating a *cross-rhythm* or *cross-meter effect*. The following example mixes patterns of threes and twos.

Right-Hand Techniques

Textures

TRACK 17

The early stride player's right-hand textures were similar to those of New Orleans jazz. Single notes, octaves, filled-in octaves, intervals, and chords were used. The chords, however, were often fuller, sometimes even spanning beyond an octave to a ninth or tenth.

Like Jelly Roll Morton, James P. Johnson often added harmony to single notes and octaves. However, Johnson more often used intervals, octaves, chords, etc. for coloristic effects. For instance, he might play an entire passage in thirds or sixths simply for the "sound" of these intervals. The following passage is dominated by filled-in sixths in the right hand.

Blues Effects

Like New Orleans piano, early stride differentiated itself from classic ragtime early on by using blues effects. James P. Johnson used several blues devices, such as blue notes, grace notes, crushed notes, etc. The following example demonstrates some of these devices.

Melodic Rhythms

While Jelly Roll Morton's melodic rhythms were somewhat rooted in classic ragtime, James P. Johnson's were closer to pure jazz. The following rhythms are taken from Johnson's famous "Carolina Shout."

Call and Response

Call-and-response passages are a staple of early stride. Typically, a short rhythmic figure in a higher register acts as the "call," and then the same or a different figure in a lower register acts as the "response." Sometimes, the call is played in the right hand and the response in the left.

Rhythmic Drive and Improvisation

Early stride pianists played with an intense rhythmic drive. The left hand kept up a steady and at times extremely fast tempo. Left-hand accents were either evenly played on every beat or played on beats 2 and 4. Right-hand accents could come anywhere, and cross-rhythmic effects were typical in both hands. Like early New Orleans pianists, the early stride players improvised through ornamentation and variation.

"Shoo Fly Shout"

"Shoo Fly Shout" is a fast shout written in James P. Johnson's style. Its sectional form is modeled after classic ragtime and consists of five strains arranged as: Intro, AABBCDEE, Coda. Each strain is sixteen measures long.

Notice the variety of left-hand techniques, including stride, walking bass, and displaced accents. Notice the cross-rhythm effect in the left hand during the B and C sections and offbeat accents in both hands during the D section. The E strains act as "shout choruses" and feature call-and-response patterns. E1 is a variation on the E section, done in a way that might have been improvised.

John Valerio

PRACTICE SUGGESTIONS

Practice typical early stride/James P. Johnson progressions—stepwise and otherwise. Remember that these usually were played at very fast tempos. An example follows.

- Choose segments from "Shoo Fly Shout" and improvise a new left-hand part.

- Improvise typical Johnson melodies, including call-and-response patterns, while playing an early stride-like left-hand part.

- Refer to some of Johnson's compositions like "Carolina Shout" and "Charleston."

Chapter Five

STRIDE PIANO II
FATS WALLER

Stride playing evolved rapidly during the 1920s. The harmonic language became more sophisticated, and the overall sound became smoother and somewhat softer. The most popular and influential later stride pianist was **Fats Waller** (1904-1943). Strongly influenced by James P. Johnson who tutored him in the stride style, Waller was classically trained and possessed a virtuoso technique. His touch was lighter than Johnson's, and he serves as a transitional figure between stride style and the lighter swing style of the 1930s and '40s.

Waller had a certain refinement in his technique that was not apparent in Johnson's playing. A prolific composer who wrote hundreds of pop songs—including "Ain't Misbehavin'," "Honeysuckle Rose," and "This Joint Is Jumpin'"—Waller was also a successful entertainer, a popular singer, and a comedian. Although he died at an early age due to overindulgence in food and drink, he left a legacy of hundreds of recordings. Waller recorded with a trio and small groups, but his output consists mostly of solo piano recordings.

Left-Hand Techniques

Later stride used all basic left-hand techniques of early stride—the left hand kept the pulse as before and bass-note/chord alternation was still the norm, with occasional walking bass lines and melodic passages—but, of course, added some new twists. A typical passage follows.

Chords

Notice the richer chords in the example above. While triads were still used in later stride, seventh and sixth chords became commonplace. Fuller textures were more popular, and chord voicings often contained four notes, as opposed to just three. Extended harmonies—ninth, eleventh, and thirteenth chords—were also employed on occasion.

Following are some common major sixth voicings. These were often used in place of major triads, but not always. (The triad voicings shown in Chapter 1 were still employed by stride pianists.)

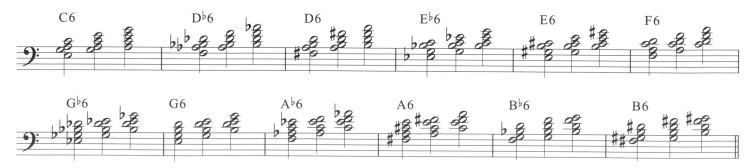

Voicings for dominant seventh chords were similar to those used by Jelly Roll Morton and can be applied to all seventh chords—m7, m7♭5, and °7. (Maj7 chords were not as common.)

As in early stride, stepwise bass lines were increasingly common. Notice the unusual inversions/chord tones in this bass line, as well as the smooth voice leading.

Bass Notes

Other than single notes and octaves, later stride pianists also used tenths, fifths, and tenths filled in with fifths, sixths, or sevenths for bass notes (more so than in New Orleans jazz).

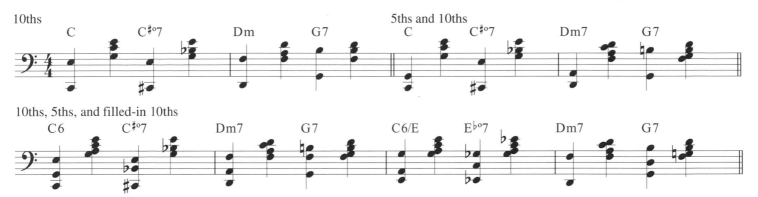

Tenths

During the later stages of stride's evolution, tenths became more prominent in the left hand. A *tenth* is a compound interval that is essentially a displaced third; when the upper note of a third is displaced an octave higher, or the bottom note an octave lower, a tenth is formed. For harmonic reasons, only certain tenths are used to imply individual chord qualities and inversions. Two basic rules can be followed in choosing tenths for the left hand:

1. Major tenths = major or dominant seventh chords

Due to the strong overtone relationship of a major third, the major tenth suggests the root and third of a major or dominant chord. It should not be used for other chord types (e.g., as the third and fifth of a minor chord).

2. Minor tenths = any chord type

Minor tenths can imply root position minor or diminished chords, as well as inversions of various chords—including major and dominant.

Based on these rules, the tenths that can be used for each chord quality are as follows.

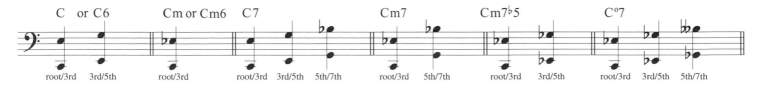

Of course, a single tenth can imply several different chords; for instance, the tenth D–F could be interpreted as follows.

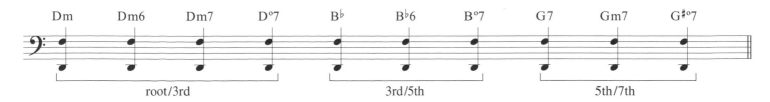

Tenths can be difficult to play for pianists with small- to average-size hands. Minor tenths are possible for most players; major tenths can be more problematic. Tenths can be broken down into four levels of difficulty.

When a tenth is out of reach, the player can *roll* it—playing the lower or upper note of the tenth as a grace note before the other note. Stride players did this often as an effect, anyway.

TRACK 22

This is similar to the "broken tenth" effect described later. Although it's a workable solution to the large span problem, one should be careful not to overdo this effect. Instead, one can avoid a tenth if necessary and play a single note, octave, or fifth. (See also Chapter 6.)

Filled-In Tenths

As noted previously, tenths can be filled in; the resulting three-note structure could be a triad or imply a seventh chord. The additional note usually removes the ambiguity regarding the intended chord, and inversions are more clearly implied. The prohibition against using the open major tenth for inversions is removed when the middle note clarifies the intended chord. Below are some possibilities for major and minor tenths.

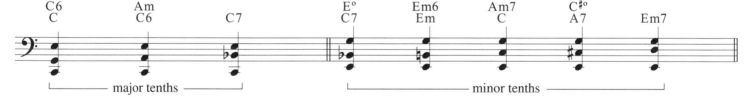

Left-Hand Patterns

Stride pianists sought variety in their left-hand playing and discovered countless ways of presenting the basic "oom-pah" pattern. The use of alternative bass-note aggregates and richer chords allowed for a more diverse textural and sonic palette. Following are some of the many ways that a I or IV chord (typically a major triad or major sixth) can be played for one measure.

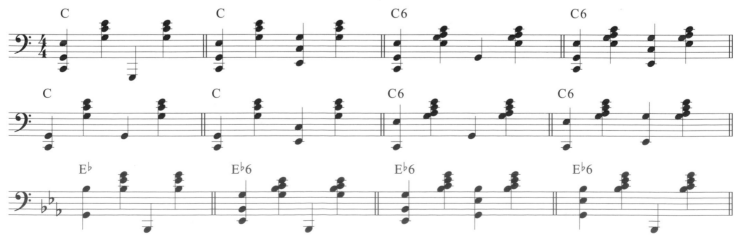

Following are some one-measure patterns for V chords (dominant sevenths).

Walking Bass

Fats Waller used a variety of textures to create walking bass passages. He and other later stride players went beyond the older technique of playing single notes or octaves; they also used tenths and filled-in tenths. The following example shows a typical use of "walking tenths."

In the previous excerpt, the tenths on the second and third beats of the second measure are treated as passing tones. Each tenth, however, could be considered as an individual chord. The choice could be determined by what the right hand is playing, or simply by personal perception. When walking tenths are filled in with middle notes, individual chords are more obviously intended. Two examples follow.

Broken Tenths

Waller used an interesting device that broke tenths into separate notes. The first note could be the lower or upper note of the tenth and acts as a kind of grace note or anticipation tied over to the second note. Two examples follow.

Continuous Chords

Sometimes, Waller played a series of chords without the interrupting bass notes. This device was typically used for very quick tempos.

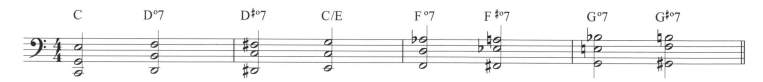

Stride pianists sometimes played open and filled-in tenths or other chord voicings as half notes or whole notes. Although this disrupts the basic quarter-note pulse, it is done for two reasons: 1) it can provide relief from the constant playing of quarter notes, and 2) it frees the middle register for the right hand to play melodic material in that range.

Boogie Woogie Patterns

TRACK 24

Waller often used boogie woogie patterns within a performance. Simple boogie woogie patterns added textural and rhythmic variety to the music. A few samples follow.

Right-Hand Techniques

Fats Waller incorporated all of the right-hand techniques of James P. Johnson but also played in a more modern style. His approach was lighter than Johnson's and a bit more horizontal or linear in general. Waller was an outstanding pop songwriter who wrote and played catchy, singable melodies. His melodies were based more on pop music than on ragtime or early jazz.

Textures

TRACK 25

Waller used the full gamut of right-hand textures, from single notes and octaves to rich, dense chords. As with Jelly Roll Morton and James P. Johnson, he could use chords to accent predominately single-note lines.

TRACK 26

Waller also used intervals or fuller harmonies for variety. Sometimes, entire passages were played with one texture predominating. The following example demonstrates how different textures can change the sound of a melody. The same two-measure passage is presented first in single notes, then in sixths, filled-in sixths, fourths and fifths, octaves, and filled-in octaves.

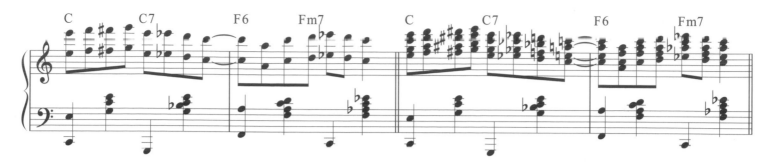

Motives

Waller's playing and compositions are replete with motives. A *motive* is a short melodic, rhythmic, or melodic/rhythmic idea that gets used in various ways. A motive can serve as a source idea that's manipulated and changed throughout a composition. Sometimes entire melodies are derived from a basic simple idea. Motives are usually "catchy" and easy to remember. Waller used motives both in obvious and subtle ways. Following are the melodic rhythms for two of Waller's best-known songs. Notice how rhythmic motives are employed.

Grace Notes and Trills

TRACK 27

Waller often used trills and grace notes as ornamental devices. He derived these not only from the blues piano tradition, but from classical piano as well. Four excerpts follow.

Runs

Occasionally, Waller interspersed quick runs among his melodic lines. These were usually based on pentatonic scales or arpeggios. Two examples follow.

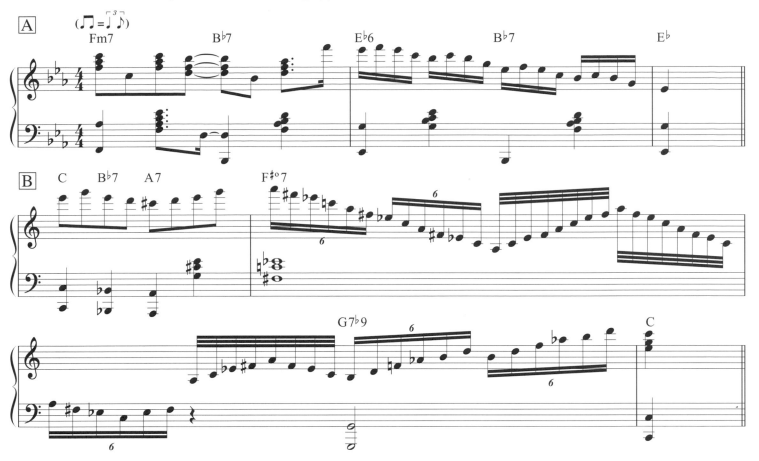

The use of runs became a staple of swing piano styles. See Chapters 7 and 8 for more on runs.

Two-Hand Techniques

Waller occasionally broke from the quarter-note pulse to create chordal passages with both hands, octaves with both hands, or counter-melodies in the left hand. The following excerpt displays chords and octaves with both hands. Notice the dominant ninth voicings.

The next excerpt displays a left-hand counter-melody followed by octaves in both hands.

Reharmonization

Stride pianists shied away from exact repetition. Typically, they reharmonized repeated melodic passages. The trick to doing this is relatively simple. Reduce the chord progression down to its essential harmonic goals—typically I or V—and fit chords that will not conflict with the melody in between the goals. One should be aware of temporary modulations and treat new tonics as I chords, etc. The following example shows various ways of going from I to V within a two-measure span.

More examples of reharmonization will be shown in Chapters 7 and 8.

Improvisation

Waller improvised constantly, but mostly through variation and ornamentation. His improvisations were more modern than James P. Johnson's in that he played off the chords more by using arpeggios and runs. Examples of his approach will be demonstrated in the following tunes.

"Misbelievin'"

TRACK 31

"Misbelievin'" is a medium tempo tune in the standard AABA pop song format. Each A section is a different variation on the same melody. Notice the textural variety—from single notes to open thirds and sixths, to filled-in sixths, to octaves and filled-in octaves. Also, notice the runs. The left hand, with its use of tenths, differs considerably from early stride style.

John Valerio

"Be Fat Blues"

"Be Fat Blues" is a medium tempo blues in Fats Waller's style. There are three choruses, each a different variation on the same melody. Notice the use of typical blues devices such as grace notes, blue notes, parallel thirds and fourths. The variation procedure demonstrates Waller's improvisational approach. Notice the use of boogie woogie devices in the left hand as well as standard stride procedures.

TRACK 32

"Mouthful of Peas"

"Mouthful of Peas" is an up-tempo shout. It has aspects of earlier as well as later stride. It contains two choruses in an AABA pop song format. The second chorus is typical of Waller's improvisational style based on variation and ornamentation. Notice the use and manipulation of the opening motive. Notice the walking bass lines in the left hand. Notice the shout-like chorus effect with full, accented chords in the right hand during the last A section.

TRACK 33

John Valerio

"Ain't Nobody"

"Ain't Nobody" is a moderately slow ballad in Waller's style, in an AABA pop song form. It features counter-melodies and boogie woogie patterns in the left hand along with basic stride patterns. Notice the full two-hand sonorities and walking open and filled-in tenths. During the last A section, the right hand plays a variation based on chord arpeggios.

TRACK 34

John Valerio

PRACTICE SUGGESTIONS

Practice progressions from any of the pop standards of the 1920s and '30s in a Fats Waller style, using tenths as striding bass notes and walking bass lines. Some examples of typical opening and turnaround progressions follow. Practice these in several keys.

Improvise Waller-like left- and right-hand parts. Play melodies from various pop standards by isolating a single texture, then combine these with single-note textures, as demonstrated by the Waller-like arrangements in this chapter. Fill in spaces with runs.

Chapter Six

SWING PIANO I
TEDDY WILSON

Early jazz had always been evolving on two simultaneous fronts—as a small ensemble music, and as a solo piano music. By the mid 1930s, ensembles were changing. Jazz bands were growing larger, into "big bands"—essentially, hybrids of the jazz combos and larger dance bands of the '20s. Along with the transition from smaller to larger groups, a "smoothing out" process took place in the music, and a distinctly new piano style emerged.

One crucial defining characteristic of swing* music is the evenness of all four beats played by the rhythm section. The rhythm sections of the big bands used a bassist who usually played on all four beats of the measure, laying down an even 4/4. This was different from the tuba or bass players of older New Orleans style, who usually played on beats 1 and 3, with occasional walking fills. The epitome of a swing rhythm section was Count Basie's band; they played all four beats of each measure with such evenness and precision they sound like one person.

Swing pianists were caught between two worlds. Still rooted in the stride/ragtime model, they began exploring new ways to establish the 4/4 pulse while freeing up the left hand. Swing demanded a lighter touch and a looser feel; the driving accents of stride piano were ironed out. Although the left hand still relied on an oom-pah striding motion, dynamic levels became more consistent for bass notes and after-chords. So-called "walking bass" lines became commonplace.

The consummate swing pianist was **Teddy Wilson** (1912-1986). His playing represents the highest cultivation of the pure swing style. Balance and restraint characterize his approach. Classically trained, Wilson had a refined sense of touch. His technique was supple, and his music, subtle. One reason for the lighter touch of the swing pianists was the use of the microphone; the earlier jazz pianists had to pound on the piano to be heard within a group setting. Wilson gained notoriety when he teamed up with clarinetist Benny Goodman and drummer Gene Krupa to form the Benny Goodman Trio. This group was historically important not only for the great music they created but also for being the first publicized interracial jazz performing group. The fact that this trio had no bass player is a testament to Wilson's astounding left-hand technique and conception. Wilson played solo piano in much the same way as he approached playing with a group.

*The term *swing* as used here refers to the style of jazz that evolved from the mid 1930s to the mid '40s. It should not be confused with the more general use of the word denoting the rhythmic conception associated with most jazz.

Left-Hand Techniques

Most of the left-hand techniques used by swing pianists were already used by the late stride players. As with earlier styles, the left hand mostly kept time by playing the quarter-note pulse. Crucial differences were that now all of the beats were played with equal stress, the touch was much lighter, and the feeling was more relaxed. The hard-driving left hand of the stride pianists was replaced by a steady, relaxed groove. There was also a difference in when and how often the swing pianists applied each left-hand technique. These newer approaches are described in the following pages.

Chords

Swing pianists increased the upper range of chords slightly. The basic range was between E below middle C to C above middle C. They essentially used the same chords as the later stride pianists but added more ninths (natural and flatted).

While the seventh and sixth chord positions used by the earlier jazz pianists were still common, in keeping with the lighter approach of swing piano, Teddy Wilson often played just fragments of chords or even just one note for "after-chords." Below are examples for some of the fragment voicings favored by Teddy Wilson.

One can derive similar voicings for minor sixth, minor seventh, and minor seventh flat-five chords. Wilson rarely used major seventh chords.

Bass Notes

Swing pianists used the same intervals and chords for "bass notes" as the later stride pianists; however, in swing, the softer sound of the open tenth was clearly favored over single notes and octaves. A typical segment of a swing piano left-hand part follows.

Other common bass notes include fifths, sixths, sevenths, and filled-in tenths used for triads or seventh chords. An example from Teddy Wilson follows.

Since the swing style is based on evenness of the pulse, rolling a hand to reach the tenth generally is not as desirable as it is in stride style. Although this is acceptable on occasion, an alternative solution is to drop the lowest note and play the top note by itself. Swing pianists sometimes did this anyway for musical effect (see Tenor Lines).

Walking Tenths

Swing pianists played walking bass lines in tenths, as their predecessors had, but with more regularity; sometimes, walking lines dominated entire sections of the music. Most lines were stepwise, but small skips were occasionally used. In keeping with the style, these lines were played very evenly, devoid of accents.

Three types of walking lines were common: diatonic, chromatic, and mixed. Diatonic stepwise motion is very useful for connecting notes a fifth apart, as in the following two examples.

To connect smaller intervallic spans, chromatic motion is usually required. Below are examples for connecting notes a fourth, third, and second apart.

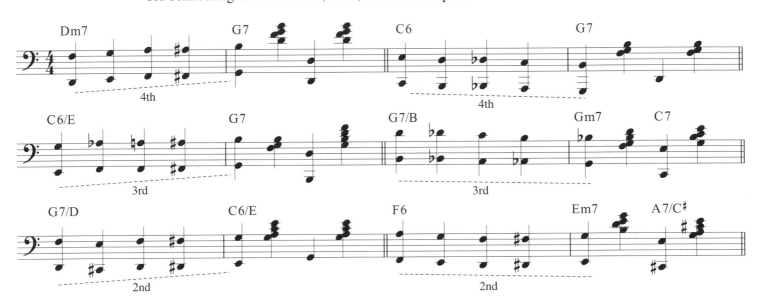

Walking tenths are also used to "circle back" on a note.

Most walking lines were one measure in length; but longer spans also occurred. Sometimes walking tenths continue for two or more measures. Two examples follow.

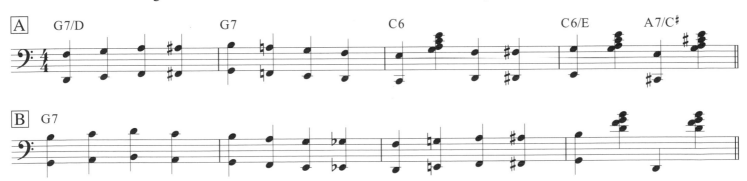

Harmonic Prolongation

Harmonic prolongation refers to the elaboration of a single chord through harmonic motions away from and back to that chord. Typically in swing, this is accomplished through a combination of walking tenths and oom-pah striding. As previously mentioned, the harmonic implications of open tenths can be determined in context with the right hand. (Although there is no right hand in the following examples, implied harmonies are indicated by the chord symbols.)

Four-measure prolongation of a I chord (C6) is demonstrated here, moving to Dm7.

Two-measure prolongation of a I chord is shown here (four examples).

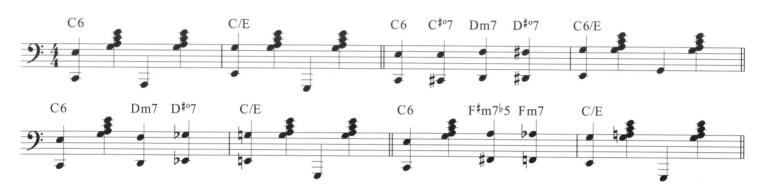

Walking Chords

Filled-in tenths can be used for walking lines as the later stride players used them. An example from Teddy Wilson follows. Notice here that each beat represents a distinct chord change.

Half-Note Chords

Swing pianists sometimes played open and filled-in tenths as half notes. Although this disrupts the basic quarter-note pulse, it was done for two reasons: 1) to avoid monotony, and 2) to free the middle register for the right hand to play melodic material in that range.

Single-Note and Two-Note Afterbeats

As previously mentioned, Wilson often used chord fragments or single notes instead of full after-chords. This was especially true in up-tempo performances. One simple but effective device is based on open or filled-in tenths: Play the bottom note of the tenth as a bass note and the top note (or notes) as an "after-chord."

TRACK 35

Sometimes the left hand played a series of single notes, either as a bass line or modified stride.

Tenor Lines

TRACK 36

Wilson often brought out a middle voice in his playing. He did this by sustaining the upper notes in the left hand while playing staccato lower notes to keep the pulse going. The sustained tenor line that resulted added a third line in counterpoint to the melody and bass lines.

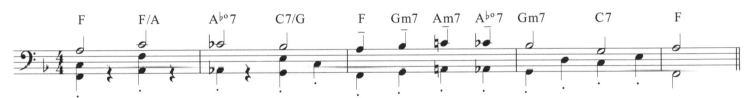

TRACK 37

Notice in the next excerpt that the bass line drops out in the third measure while the tenor line continues.

TRACK 38

Constructing tenor lines is a good way to avoid playing difficult tenths. By dropping the bass out but keeping the tenor line going, one can maintain the pulse without losing much continuity. In the example below, large spans on the E♭6 and A♭ chords are avoided by dropping the bass out.

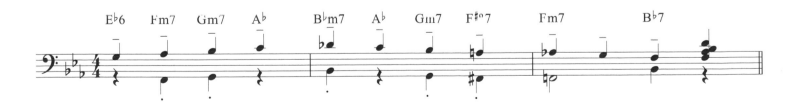

Left-Hand Variety

Teddy Wilson's left-hand style was based on variety. Most measures differed from those preceding and following. Bass notes, after-chords, chord voicings, textures, etc. were always changing. Motion is constant and continuous, and the lack of sameness keeps the listener and the player on his toes. A typical excerpt follows.

TRACK 39

Right-Hand Techniques

Textures

TRACK 40

Like the stride players, Teddy Wilson used a combination of single notes, octaves, filled-in octaves, chords, and intervals in his right-hand melodies. However, he used many more single notes; this went along with the lighter, more fluid approach of the swing style. Wilson favored an evenness of line that made his lines more subtle and supple than those of the stride pianists.

Runs

Runs were essential to swing; Teddy Wilson often interspersed his melodic lines with dazzling descending and ascending runs. As in stride, they were mostly based on pentatonic scales and chord arpeggios. Often, however, more advanced chordal structures were used in swing.

Pentatonic

Essentially, there were three kinds of pentatonic scales used during the Swing period: major, minor, and dominant. Major pentatonic scales were used on major and dominant chords; minor pentatonic scales were used on minor chords; and dominant pentatonic scales were used on dominant seventh chords. These three pentatonic scales from the tonic C follow.

TRACK 41

Following are four excerpts of pentatonic runs from Teddy Wilson.

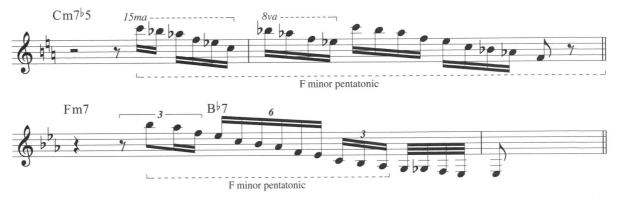

Arpeggios & Fragments

Wilson often arpeggiated chords and chord fragments for runs. Two full arpeggio runs follow.

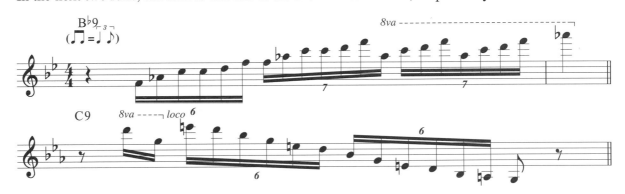

In the next two runs, the root is left out of the B♭9 and C9 chords, respectively.

Other Scales & Sounds

Various scales were used for runs. This excerpt uses whole-tone and chromatic scale fragments.

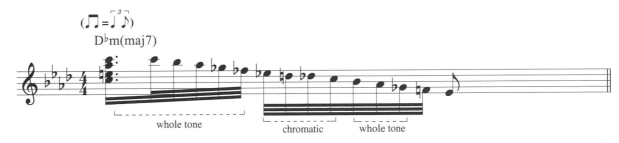

Arpeggiated fourths create a more exotic sound. Two excerpts follow.

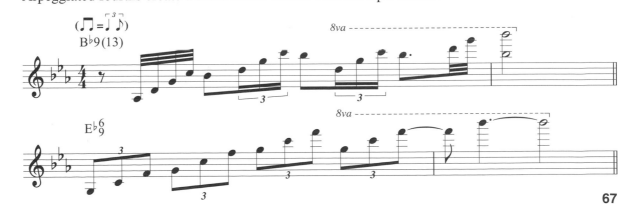

Tremolos

Wilson often played octaves by rapidly alternating both notes as a *tremolo*. (Any alternation of two notes wider than a second is called a "tremolo"; alternating seconds are called "trills.") Wilson's use of octave tremolos can be traced to Earl Hines, who used this device in his famous "trumpet style" piano playing dating back to the 1920s. Tremolo chords were used, also.

TRACK 46

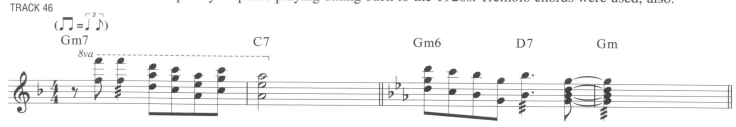

Improvisation

While most jazz improvisors prior to the Swing era relied on ornamentation and variation of given material, most swing pianists created truer improvisations by playing more off of the chord changes rather than the melody. (Louis Armstrong paved the way for this kind of improvisational approach in the 1920s, as did Earl Hines.) Wilson created new melodies to the tunes he played, choosing scalar and arpeggiated lines that fit with the prevailing chords.

During I and IV chords (usually major sixths, major sevenths, or major triads), the improvised melodies consisted primarily of strict diatonic material that clearly defined the chord, with occasional passing tones. Several excerpts on an E♭6 chord follow.

TRACK 47

TRACK 48

Dominant chords were often arpeggiated within the improvised melodic line.

TRACK 49

The harmonic vocabulary of swing was more advanced than that of stride, and more seventh and ninth chords became commonplace. For Wilson, dominant chords often invited chromatic lines.

TRACK 50

Wilson sometimes played sequential-like lines over one, two, or more chords.

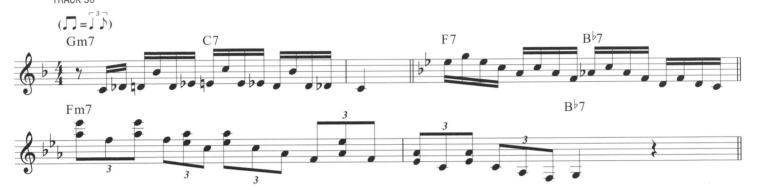

TRACK 51

Another of Wilson's favorite devices is a descending chromatic motion of three or more notes followed by a jump up a sixth or higher. Three excerpts follow.

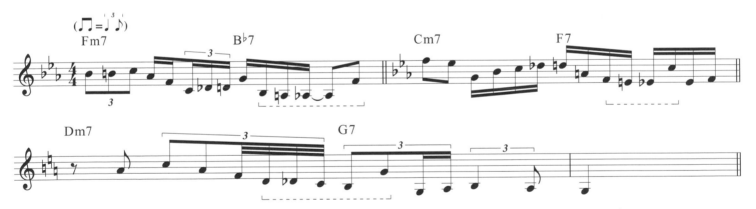

The subtle evenness of the quarter-note pulse in swing allowed for a very flexible right hand that played a variety of rhythms rather than consistent rhythmic values. This rather supple, flexible melodic style is quite different from the latter bebop style that featured long streams of eighth notes. Another Wilson example follows.

TRACK 52

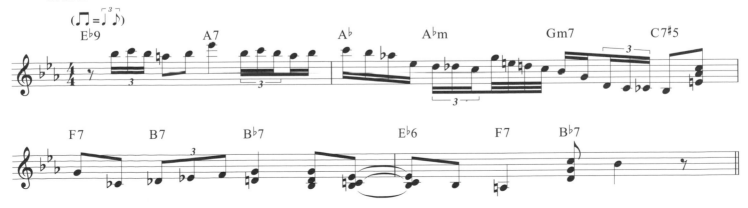

"If I've Been Had"

"If I've Been Had" is medium swing tune in a typical AABA pop song form, arranged in Teddy Wilson's style. It features many Wilson-style runs and typical left-hand devices. Notice the walking tenths and tenor lines in the left hand. The second chorus is an improvisation on the first, and demonstrates some of Wilson's improvisational techniques.

TRACK 53

John Valerio

"Remind Me"

"Remind Me" is a medium ballad in AABA pop song form, arranged in Teddy Wilson's style. The right plays continuous variations and improvisations during the A sections. Notice the runs, tenor lines, and walking tenths.

TRACK 54

John Valerio

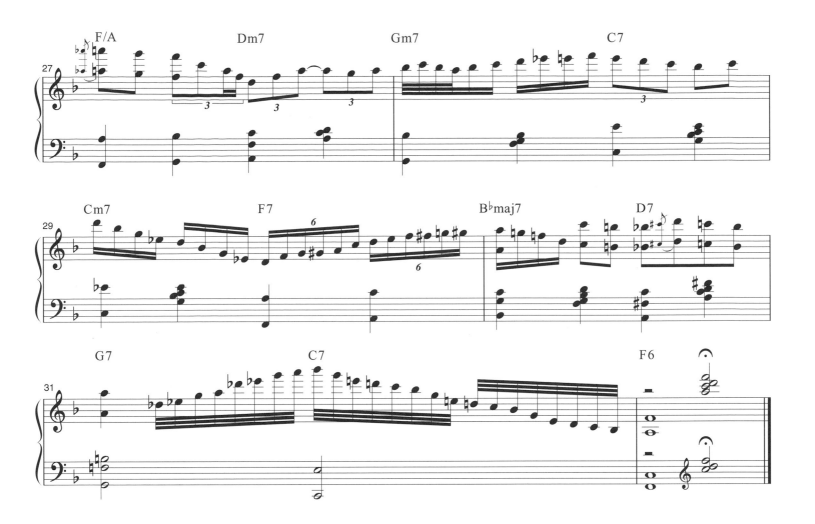

"Light and Bright"

"Light and Bright" is an up-tempo, stripped down swing tune in an AABA form. It features a simplified left-hand stride with mostly single notes based on broken tenths, and occasional walking tenths. The right hand plays mostly single notes. This is an exercise in fast swing playing without the extras.

TRACK 55

John Valerio

PRACTICE SUGGESTIONS

Practice walking tenths to progressions from pop standards from the 1930s and '40s. An example of dominant chords going down the complete circle of fifths follows. For difficult tenths, the bass note (in parentheses) may be dropped out.

Practice basic intros and turnarounds by combining walking tenths with striding patterns.

Practice pentatonic ascending and descending runs. Art Tatum fingered pentatonic and other runs with his first three fingers only. Examples for C and E♭ major pentatonic scales follow.

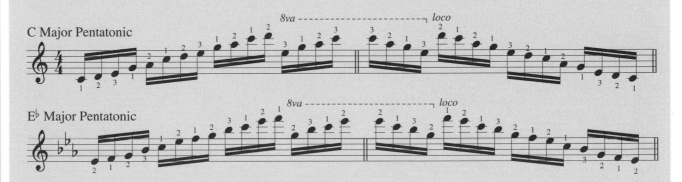

Apply similar fingering for all pentatonic runs. Practice diatonic scale and arpeggio runs.

Practice improvising in the right hand in Teddy Wilson's style while playing a steady beat in the left hand. Play some pop standards and apply various Wilson techniques in both hands.

Chapter Seven

SWING PIANO II
ART TATUM

Although Teddy Wilson best represents the swing style, **Art Tatum** (1910-1956) summed up the entire history of jazz piano and in many ways pointed the way to future, inspiring the next generation of jazz musicians, the bebop players. One of the most remarkable musicians who ever lived, Tatum was virtually blind yet possessed such dazzling technique that many illustrious classical pianists held him in awe. But his brilliance was not just a matter of technical prowess. Tatum's harmonic conception was singular: He reharmonized tunes in unexpected ways and often wrote or improvised ingenious chord progressions that amazed his contemporaries. Tatum's playing was still somewhat rooted in the ragtime model, but he took jazz piano further than anyone before him. He played sometimes with a trio, but the majority of his recordings are solo performances.

Left-Hand Techniques

Tatum used all of the left-hand techniques of stride and swing and added several of his own. The following excerpt (from a recording of "Tea for Two") shows Tatum's approach to the basic stride "oom-pah" left hand.

- Notice the use of sevenths and filled-in sevenths for "bass notes." Also, notice the use of ninths. Tatum routinely used these intervals as bass notes, along with the other intervals more typical of other stride and swing players.
- The eighth-note "kick" on the "and" of beat 4 in measure 2 is also typical of Tatum.
- The after-beat chords are similar to those used by Teddy Wilson, with the exception of the major seventh chord, which Wilson rarely used.
- The walking filled-in tenths demonstrate Tatum's penchant for fuller left-hand harmonies. He was prone to use them more often that the open tenths favored by Wilson.

Tenth Voicings

Tatum made much use of full "tenth chords"—i.e., voicings that span a tenth and contain all four notes of a seventh chord—as bass notes in a striding left hand or as walking bass. In root position, this is accomplished by displacing the third to the tenth while keeping the fifth and seventh. The basic seventh chords with the root C can be voiced as full tenth chords as follows.

Diatonic "tenth" chords in the keys of C major and F major are shown below.

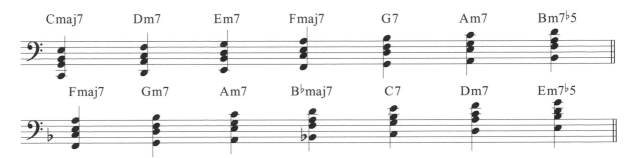

Tatum also used inversions of these voicings. Thus, each chord could be played in four positions. A C7 with all inversions is shown below. Note that the third inversion spans the interval of a ninth rather than a tenth.

Needless to say, these voicings can be difficult if not impossible for the average pianist. Leaving a note out of the middle of any of the voicings can render them more playable. Tatum himself did this more often than playing the full versions. With this system, we can arrive at sixteen different voicings for each chord. Below are all the possibilities for a C7.

A typical Tatum series of tenth chords is shown in the following excerpt. (Notice the eighth-note "kick" to beat 3 in measure 4.)

Double Time

TRACK 56

Tatum often doubled the speed of his left hand, as well as his right. Below is an excerpt of a sudden *double time* passage in the left hand. Tatum was apt to suddenly shift into and out of double time.

Voice Leading (Dyads)

In place of a full chord, Tatum often played just two notes in his left hand (again, as "bass notes" in a stride or as a walking bass). He connected these dyads through a simple voice-leading principle. In tonal music, the most common chord root movement is down by a fifth, following the circle of descending fifths; thus, G moves to C, which moves to F, which moves to B♭, etc. The inner-voice movement in such a case is either the seventh of a chord moves to the third of the next chord, or vice versa.

The next example shows how this principle works with a series of II–V progressions. Each successive root moves down by a fifth, and each of the upper notes moves from 7 to 3, to 7 to 3, and so on. Notice that the II–V progressions as units are in a cycle of descending whole steps (II–V in C, II–V in B♭, II–V in A♭, etc.).

The alternating left-hand intervals of seventh-third, seventh-third, etc. can be changed slightly by turning the third into a tenth. This was more typical of Tatum.

Since only two notes of each chord are played in the left hand, the specific chord can be ambiguous. For example, the above voicings could also imply:

- a series of dominant chords moving down by fifths (D7–G7–C7–F7–B♭7–E♭7, etc.)
- m7♭5 chords alternating with dominant sevenths (Dm7♭5–G7–Cm7♭5–F7–B♭m7♭5–E♭7, etc.)

Usually any ambiguity in the left hand is cleared up by what the right hand plays. (Two-hand voicings are described later in this chapter.)

All of the voicings in the examples above can be reversed. Below, each example starts with a root-third (or root-tenth) voicing instead of a root-seventh.

Following are three excerpts of Tatum's use of two-note voicings in the left hand.

Tatum often used sevenths as bass notes when striding the left hand. He applied the same voice leading principles by alternating the bass note sevenths with tenths, even though after-beat chords were played in between. (The first example in this chapter also offers a good example of this.)

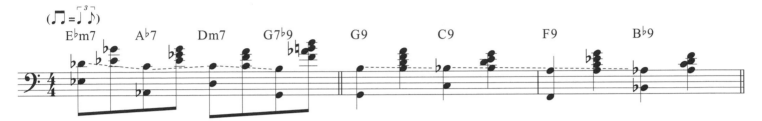

Tatum also played three-note open chord voicings in the left hand. The next example shows a descending fifth cycle of dominant chords. Notice that the same voice leading tendencies apply.

Right-Hand Techniques

Scale & Arpeggio Runs

Runs are associated with Tatum more than any other pianist, comprising a large portion of his playing; Tatum incorporated the runs of Waller and Wilson and invented many of his own.

Pentatonic

Tatum's pentatonic runs were similar to Wilson's except that Tatum often played the same pentatonic scale through several chord changes. The next two samples are both based on an E♭ major pentatonic scale. The first is played through one chord; the second, through changing chords. (See Ch. 6 for fingering ideas.)

TRACK 57

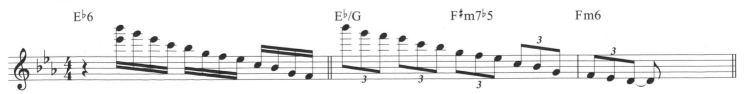

Tatum often preceded his pentatonic runs with a triplet neighboring note motion, and often ended them with chromatic scale motion. Two excerpts follow.

Two examples of dominant pentatonic runs follow. Notice the B♭ dominant pentatonic played through the II–V progression in E♭ major, as well as the chromatic inflection of the last note.

Diatonic, Whole Tone, and Hexatonic

Tatum sometimes played a descending diatonic scale as a run. This example is in C major.

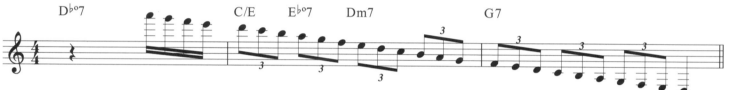

A whole tone scale is the basis for this descending run.

Hexatonic (six-note) scales were also used on occasion. Tatum's favorite was essentially a major scale minus the fourth degree. The run below begins with a chromatic scale and goes into a D♭ major hexatonic scale.

Arpeggios

Like Wilson, Tatum used incomplete chord arpeggios as runs. The first excerpt below uses 3-5-7-9 of a B♭9. The second uses 3-7-9-13 of a D9(13).

Pattern Runs

In addition to scales and arpeggios, Tatum played runs consisting of patterns—simple three- to six-note figures sequenced in rapid succession. Several types are described below.

Climbing Scale Patterns

TRACK 64

These runs consist of scale fragments repeated successively higher, usually a step at a time. The first example is a four-note ascending fragment of a C major scale.

TRACK 65

The next run uses a six-note descending pattern in a similar way. Note that here the pattern is not correlated with the beat.

G Turn Runs

TRACK 66

Many of Tatum's most impressive runs were based on patterns that lay comfortably under the fingers; these runs work primarily on specific combinations of white and black keys and are not easily transposed. For example, the following run—a turn on each note of a G major triad—is most easily played in this position with this particular fingering and works well with a G7 chord.

TRACK 67

Below is a variation. It uses triplets and leaves out one of the notes from the original run, making a double neighboring note figure. Notice the repetitive fingering.

D-Flat Runs

TRACK 68

The next set of runs work well in D♭ major. Actually, they combine D♭ major and C major scales: The thumb plays all white keys while the second and fourth fingers play a D♭ major scale in broken thirds. Notice the repetitive fingering. Several variations are shown.

Sextuplet Runs

Tatum often used sextuplets in his runs. This first run below works well with an F7 or Cm6 chord. A variation follows.

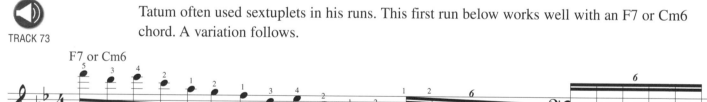

This next sextuplet run works well with a B♭7 chord.

Quintuplet Runs

Tatum also used quintuplet runs. This one uses crushed seconds and works well with an F7 chord.

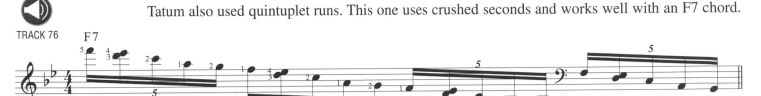

Arpeggio Patterns

Tatum often played three-note patterns based on arpeggio fragments. The example below, on an A9(13) chord, is based on the chord tones 3-5-7-9, arranged in an ascending sequence that skips the third chord tone in each grouping. (For instance, starting on beat 4, the tones played are 9-3-7, 3-5-9, 5-7-3, etc.)

A similar process is employed in this next example, based on a D♭ major triad.

There are many other characteristic runs that Tatum used, too numerous to demonstrate. Once the basic principles of his thinking in this area are grasped, one can apply these same runs to other chords and chord progressions, as well as decipher others and even invent similar runs.

Two-Hand Techniques

All of the previously described styles—from ragtime to stride to early swing—for the most part stratified the two hands into two layers of separate activity. The left hand kept the pulse and supplied the chords, while the right hand supplied the melodies along with harmonic details. Tatum did this when he wanted to, but he also played melodies in the right hand while playing chords with both hands. He integrated his two hands much more than any of the previous players. This led the way to bebop and later jazz piano styles.

Chord Voicings

Tatum's approach to playing chords with both hands was based on open left-hand voicings with filled-in notes in the right hand. The additional right-hand notes could be basic chord tones or extended and altered notes. He then superimposed melodies on top of the chord voicings.

It is easiest to categorize these two-hand voicings by the left-hand structures. There are three essential left-hand voicings: root-third (1-3), root-fifth (1-5), and root-seventh (1-7). The root-third voicing is usually played as root-tenth (1-10). This does not effect the essential structure of the voicing.

The following example shows the basic two-hand, four-note structures with root-fifth (1-5) left-hand voicings for all chord qualities on the root C. There are two versions: the first with a third-seventh (3-7) right-hand structure; the second, with seventh-third (7-3). The choice would be determined usually by the melody superimposed on top of the chord.

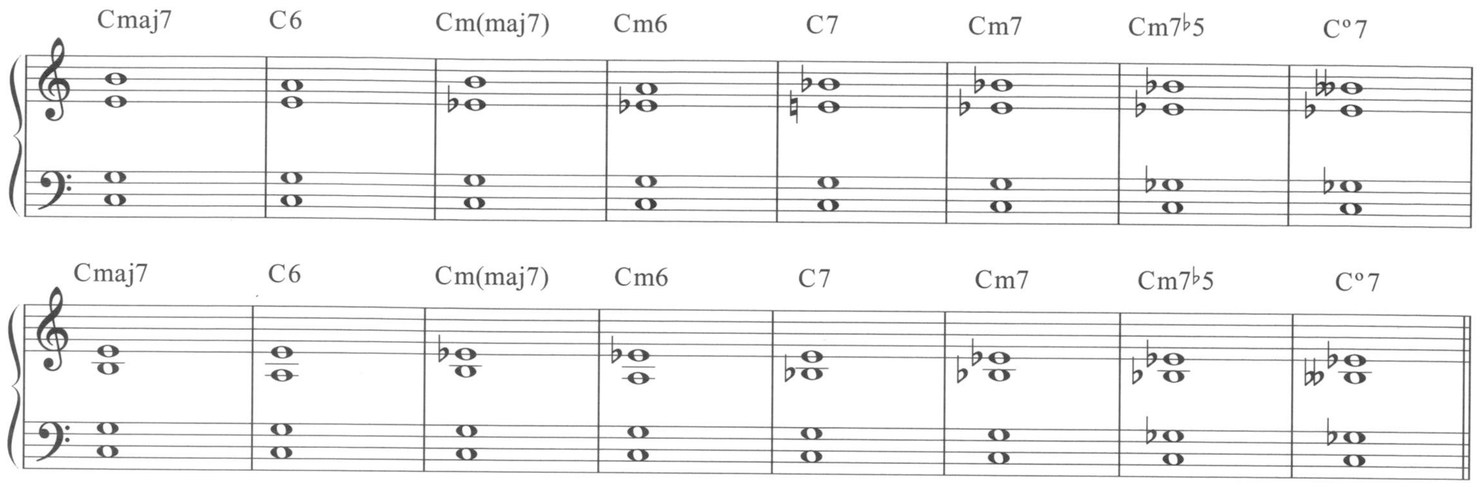

The following shows the same chords for root-seventh (1-7) left-hand structures.

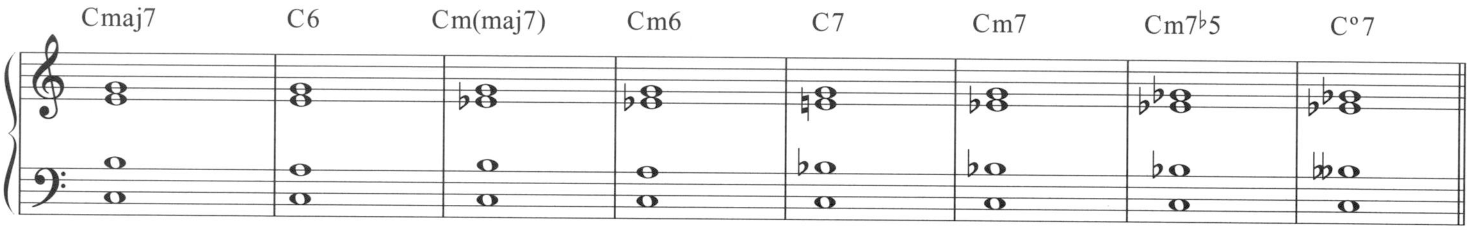

The following shows the same chords for root-tenth (1-10) left-hand structures. Notice that the ninth is added to most chords.

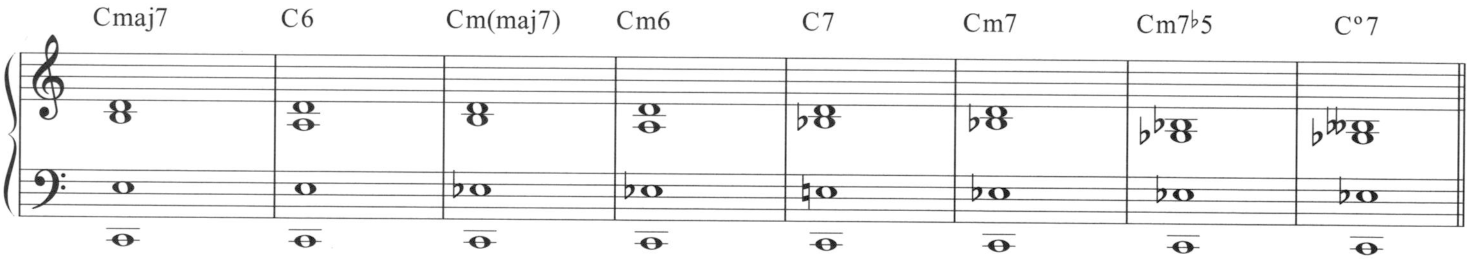

In typical circle of descending fifths progressions, 1-5-3-7 voicings can easily alternate with 1-5-7-3 voicings while maintaining a consistent open-fifths left-hand texture. II–V–I progressions in C and F major are shown below. Notice the right-hand voices alternate between the third and seventh of each chord.

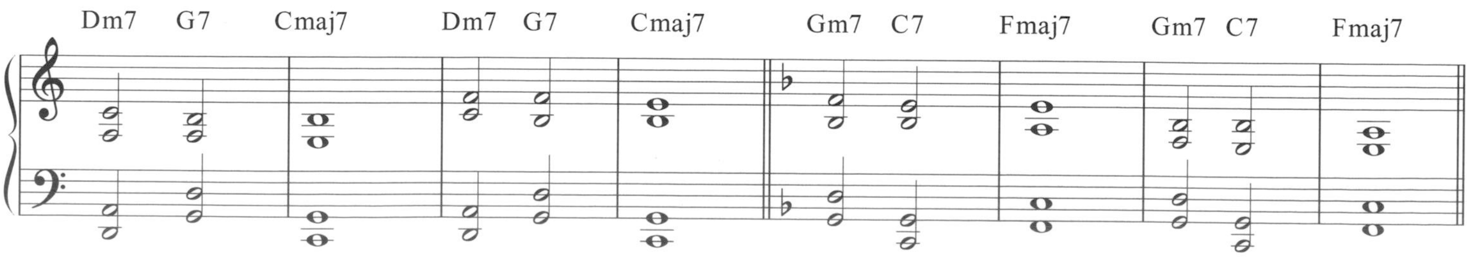

A complete cycle around the circle of descending fifths for dominant seventh chords follows.

Root-seventh (1-7) voicings often alternate with root-tenth (1-10) voicings in the left hand. The following II–V–I progressions in C and F major demonstrate how this works.

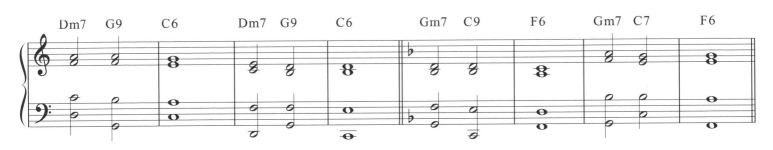

Again, a cycle of dominant seventh chords around the circle of descending fifths follows.

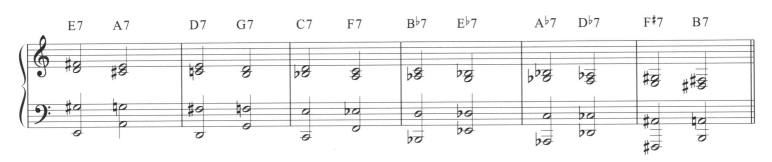

From all of the basic four-note voicings, one can derive five- to ten-note voicings as Tatum did, by adding extended, altered, and doubled chord tones. A few examples on the root C follow.

Harmonic Elaboration

Tatum was a master at harmonic elaboration, embellishment, and substitution. His innovations in these techniques directly inspired the next generation of jazz players, the bebop musicians. While early swing pianists like Teddy Wilson had used harmonic prolongation—inserting several chords where only one was typically used—Tatum took these ideas to their logical extreme, often reharmonizing every eighth note in a given passage with different chords.

Tritone Substitution

One of Tatum's favorite devices was based on the principle of *tritone substitution*. A "tritone" is an interval that spans three whole steps. The term is used to avoid confusion between the interval

of a diminished fifth and an augmented fourth, which both span the same interval but have different spellings. (A tritone inverts to a tritone, although the interval theoretically changes from one to the other.)

The principle of tritone substitution is the process of replacing one chord with another chord whose root is a tritone away. This is most commonly done with dominant chords. Therefore, a D♭7 chord

can substitute for a G7 chord, a C7 can be replaced by an F♯7, etc. A D♭7 and the G7 are not as far apart as one might think. They share two crucial notes, which happen to be a tritone apart. The third and seventh of each chord are enharmonically identical in reverse order— B and F for G7, and F and C♭ for D♭7.

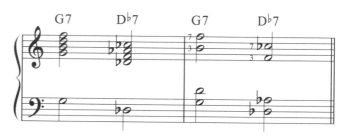

Traditionally, the third and seventh of a dominant seventh chord are the most important notes. They define the key center through their tendency to resolve to the root and third of a tonic chord. Tatum exploits the ambiguity of the tritone within a dominant seventh chord by making the two chords that share the same tritone interchangeable.

The dominant seventh tritone interchangeability is further strengthened when altered notes are used. The notes in G7b5 are enharmonically identical with those in Db7b5. Also, when a b9 is used, the top four notes of each chord are enharmonically identical. Notice that these notes form a diminished seventh chord—for tritone-related dominant b9 chords, these diminished seventh chords are enharmonically identical.

Notice that the only difference between the two chords above is the root. One can freely substitute for the other while everything else remains intact. One can see and hear the similarity of the two chords although their roots are quite different.

Fifth/Half-Step Equivalence

This brings us to the important harmonic principle of *fifth/half-step equivalence*. In any given progression involving dominant seventh chords, descending by fifth is functionally identical to descending by half step. This, of course, is possible through the principle of tritone substitution. The progressions below are all different but functionally interchangeable.

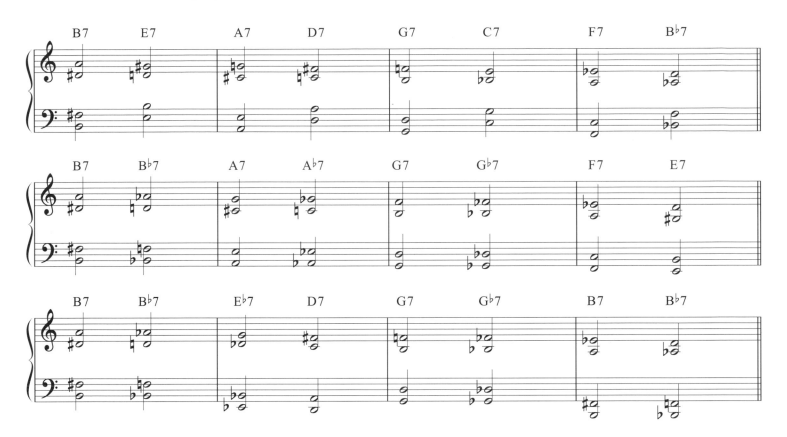

Backcycling

Tatum's reharmonizations are based mostly on circle-of-fifths progressions. The trick to doing this is to work backwards from a target chord by going through a cycle of ascending fifths. For example, if one wants to go from a C6 chord to an E7, one can approach the target chord in various ways, depending on how many intervening chords are desired.

Two-Hand Voicings & Substitution

Excerpts demonstrating the substitution techniques described follow. Notice how most voicings are derived from the basic two-handed ones shown previously. Also, notice the principle of fifth/half-step equivalence at work; these excerpts show how Tatum freely exploited this principle while creating harmonic movement within a focused tonal environment.

TRACK 79

TRACK 80

TRACK 81

TRACK 82

Improvisation

The topic of improvisation in Tatum's playing has been a controversial one. Some critics dismiss his departures from given material as mere filler, or decoration and ornamentation. They say that this is not true improvisation in the sense of creating new and original melodies on given material. While this is true for the most part, Tatum was still a remarkable improviser in that he manipulated given material in unique and creative ways. He was not a linear improviser like Teddy Wilson was, but he was much more of an improviser than Fats Waller. All of the techniques shown in this chapter—reharmonization, runs, and melodic variations—are parts of Tatum's improvisation repertoire. Close study of the arrangements of the following two tunes will give one a deeper sense of Tatum's improvisation approach.

"Off the Waterfront"

TRACK 83

"Off the Waterfront" is a tune arranged in an Art Tatum style. It is in an AABA pop song form. The arrangement contains many Tatum-like runs in both the right and left hands. Notice the variety of left-hand devices—three-note walking tenths and "bass notes," and two-hand full voicings of simpler and complex chords, along with common swing left-hand techniques. Also, notice the use of double time.

John Valerio

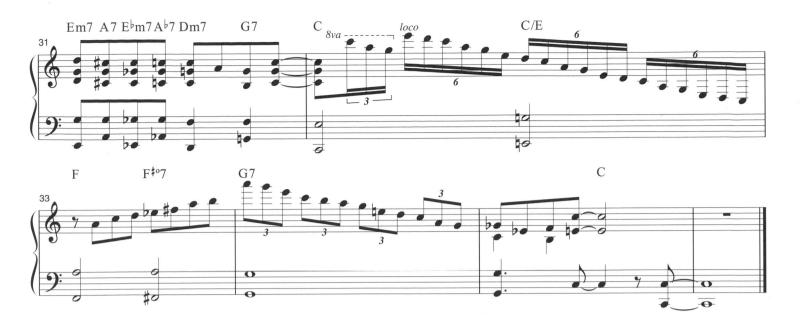

"Sunny and Soul"

"Sunny and Soul" is a ballad arranged in an Art Tatum style. It is in an AABA pop song form. It uses a variety of two-, three-, and four- note voicings in the left hand, either alone or in a striding pattern. It also contains examples of full two-hand voicings. Runs continually interrupt the tune. The basic tune is continually reharmonized, and melodic variations are used to accommodate the new harmonies.

TRACK 84

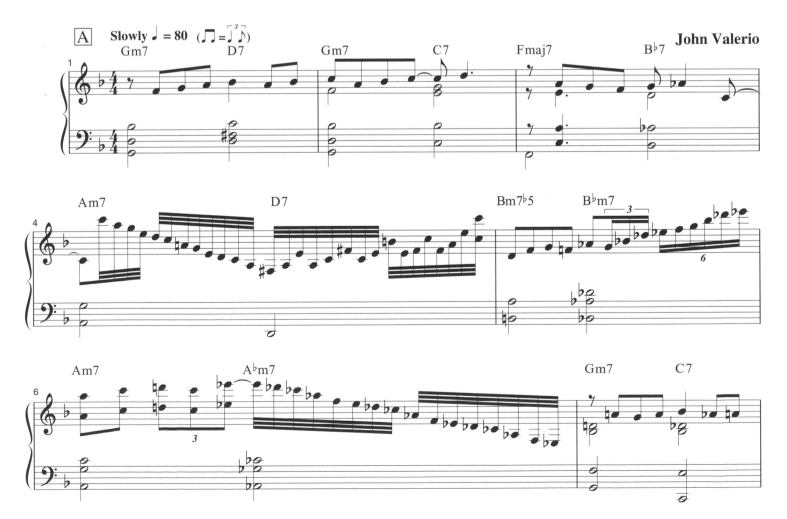

PRACTICE SUGGESTIONS

Practice walking three-note (filled-in) tenths to progressions from pop standards from the 1930s and '40s. Below are three II–V–I progressions in C, B♭, and A♭ major with walking three-note tenths implying passing chords. Practice these, and create others for more keys.

Practice striding with root-seventh and root-tenth voicings for "bass notes." Below are examples of II–V progression moving down chromatically. All after-chords are ninth chords.

Play this progression again, reversing the "bass note" voicings for each II–V unit. Thus, 1-7 becomes 1-10 and 1-10 becomes 1-7.

Practice the scale/arpeggio runs shown (pentatonic, diatonic, whole tone, hexatonic, etc.), and try similar runs on other chords and chord progressions. Also practice the key-specific pattern runs (G turn run, D♭ run, etc.) on the indicated chords and try them untransposed on other chords or progressions. These runs are specific to the finger and key patterns that they use.

Apply Tatum right-hand and left-hand techniques to any pop standard.